Three Men in the Fiery Furnace

Daniel 3
For Children
Written by Teresa Olive
Illustrated by Arthur Kirchhoff

ARCH® Books

Scripture quotations: NEW INTERNATIONAL VERSION® © 1973, 1978, 1984 by International Bible Society. Used by permission of Zondervan.

Copyright © 1994 Concordia Publishing House
3558 S. Jefferson Avenue, St. Louis, MO 63118-3968
Manufactured in the United States of America

In the land of Babylon,
 Many years ago,
There lived three men—Shadrach, Meshach,
 And Abednego.

These were men who loved the Lord.
 They worshiped Him alone,
Though other people bowed before
 False gods of wood and stone.

Then the king of Babylon
        Devised a wicked scheme.
He had a golden idol built,
        The biggest ever seen.

All the people then were told
        The king's brand-new command:
"Bow before this god of gold
        When you hear my royal band.

"If you do not bow down low
    When music starts to play,
I'll tell my guards to throw
    You in a fire without delay!"

Then the king's musicians
    Played harps and horns and flutes.
All bowed throughout the nation
    When they heard the *clangs* and *toots*.

But three men would not bow their heads
Before the god of gold.
Certain jealous leaders said,
"The king just must be told!"

They said, "Three men will not bow low
    Before your idol, sire.
Shadrach, Meshach, and Abednego
    Must go into the fire."

The three were brought before the throne.
They acted calm and brave.
They said, "We serve one God alone
And He can surely save.

"But even if He does not,
        There's one thing you should know—
Before your golden false god
        We never will bow low!"

At this, the king grew furious;
Insulted to the core.
He heated up the furnace
Much hotter than before.

To the furnace they were brought,
    And thrown, full-clothed, inside.
The blazing flames had grown so hot,
    The guards who brought them died.

The king was watching from the door.
He cried out in alarm,
"I see three men—no look! There's four
In the fire, unharmed!"

The fourth "man" was the Son of God,
Sent to save the three,
As part of God's own special plan
To set His servants free.

"Shadrach! Meshach! Abednego!"—
They heard the king's loud shout—
"Servants of the Most High God,
Will you please come out?"

The three men came out to the king.
The people crowded near,
So amazed at this strange thing,
Their knees all shook with fear.

The three men weren't hurt at all.
　　　Their clothes all looked the same.
You'd never guess that they had walked
　　　Right in the fiery flame.

"Praise the God," the king did cry,
　　　"Who rescued these three men!
They love Him and would rather die
　　　Than cease to worship Him!"

Our Father saved His servants then.
He does the same today.
He always helps His children when
They call to Him and pray.

Dear Parents:

In miraculous stories such as this one, it is easy for children to get the idea that the biblical characters are superheroes. Remind your child that God is the hero who saved Shadrach, Meshach, and Abednego from the flames. God provides the same care and protection for His children today.

Pray with your child about some problems your family is facing. Then praise God for promising to help you. As Joshua reminds us, "You know with all your heart and soul that not one of all the good promises the LORD your God gave you has failed" (Joshua 23:14).

The Editor